EASY WAYS TO BUILD ASSERTIVENESS CONFIDENCE SELF-ESTEEM

a manual for personal development
covering basic building blocks for achieving your potential

Jennie Willett

2nd edition

Jennie Willett

TSL Publications

2nd edition published in Great Britain in 2017
By TSL Publications, Rickmansworth

ISBN / 978-1-911070-62-7
1st edition (2009): ISBN / 978-1-4452-3662-9

Jennie Willett is a free-lance lecturer, trainer, therapist and writer. As a lecturer she specialises in adult teacher education, on how people learn. She also delivers personal development and management training courses for colleges and various organisations. Her voluntary work has included working with Victim Support, taking a lead on bullying issues. She has a private practice covering all areas of personal development, stress/time management and cognitive behaviour therapy.

A life without challenge is no life at all

This book is dedicated to my students
past, present and future.

Acknowledgement

Dr Peter Connell
for wise counsel, professional expertise, advice and
encouragement.

This book is based on courses I have developed on Assertiveness, Confidence and Self-esteem. The topics covered are those most requested by my students.

No two personalities are the same, therefore information and guidance given in this book is generic. It has to be the responsibility of the individual whatever choice or action they take in any given situation.

Taking responsibility is the key to self-confidence.

www.jenniewillett.co.uk

CONTENTS

HOW TO USE THIS BOOK

It is recommended that you use this book as a personal notebook. Write in it, make notes on your progress, highlight areas which are important to you.*

It is beneficial to work through the book from the beginning as each exercise builds on the next. You need to have a healthy self-esteem to be confident and you need to be confident in order to be assertive.

Buy an A4 lined pad to keep with the book to use as your personal development journal. Write daily on your progress; it can be as much or little as you wish. Most pages in the book give exercises and you can use the lined pad for these.

You will find some repetition, this is deliberate as some readers will only read parts of the book. Repetition is also used to emphasise key golden rules.

I wish you every success on your personal development journey.

Jennie Willett

*If you have borrowed this book from a library or anywhere else please do not write in it.

SELF-ESTEEM

WHAT IS SELF-ESTEEM?

It is the way we see and think about ourselves. Whether or not we like who we are, approve of who we are and accept ourselves unconditionally. That means accepting our imperfections.

Self-esteem is formed between the ages of 0-6. Some will say it is partly formed whilst in the womb. Certain aspects of our self-esteem may be in our genes and that is where the argument nature or nurture comes into question.

Some self-esteem may be genetic. The rest will be formed in accordance with the environment in which a child lives their formative years. If children live in an emotionally secure and safe environment with a balance of praise and discipline, knowing they are loved unconditionally, then they should grow to acquire a healthy self-esteem.

For children raised by those with a low self-esteem, it is inevitable they will emulate the behaviour. If there is a lack of praise and support with an imbalance of discipline, fairness plus inappropriate treatment then children may display a low sense of self-worth with emotions such as anger, fear and guilt. They will grow to be judgemental in their view of themselves, aiming for perfection in order to be liked.

Regularly I am asked the question *can I improve my self-esteem as an adult?* Although we may not be able to change totally behaviour learnt in childhood, we can learn new skills in how to accept who we are and how to be confident in our values and core-beliefs. We can learn how either to change them or build on them. At times we may revert to our default mechanism but we can learn to cope with relapses as will be explained further in the book.

When first reading a self-help book, the information goes into the short-term memory. By doing the recommended exercises the information transfers into the long-term memory.

TYPICAL CAUSES OF LOW SELF-ESTEEM

- Continual criticism.
- Being disciplined in an accusative manner: *you naughty child*. No one, child or adult, learns from being *told off*. Children learn to label themselves with the language used by those around them (stupid, clumsy, idiot, fat, shy).
- Being laughed at.
- Sarcasm.
- Over anxious parents/guardians.
- Over protective parents/guardians.
- Parents with low self-esteem.
- Being ridiculed.
- Bullying.
- Being raised in an environment of fear, tension, anger, guilt and shame.
- Not being as good as/or compared with siblings.
- Not listened to.
- Opinions dismissed.
- Being shouted at.
- Abused verbally and or physically.
- Lack of praise, encouragement and support.

In her poem *Children Learn What They Live*, Dorothy Law Nolte explains how self-esteem is formed. See the poem at: empowermentresources.com.

SELF-ESTEEM BUILDING IN THE FORMATIVE YEARS

The atmosphere in which children live on a daily basis will have a direct impact on their self-esteem.

Children living with adults who continually argue may grow up with a view that such behaviour is acceptable. They learn the views and beliefs of those around them; if they experience certain attitudes, for example racism or sexism, they are likely to accept those beliefs as the norm.

Children who are bullied can grow up to be either bullies or victims of further bullying.

Children who grow up in a loving and caring environment with role models for good manners, respect and thought for others will emulate that behaviour. What children experience everyday will become their script for life:

- Encouragement.
- Tolerance.
- Support.
- Acceptance and approval.
- Truth and honesty.
- Kindness.
- Empathy.
- Laughter.
- Integrity.
- Security.

Children need roots and wings.

The language and tone of voice used to children is important. If we label children, they will grow up with those labels. Continually tell a child they are a genius and they will believe it. Continually tell a child they are stupid and they will believe that too. Both of these extremes could cause problems in later life.

If children hear bad language at home they will deem it acceptable to use that language. Parents and guardians are role models.

It needs to be stressed that in the main, parents and guardians do the best they know how at the time. They may have been parented in the same way and go on to parent in the same way. To apportion blame and be non-forgiving will hamper self-development.

Let go, accept, move on with the help of this book. This will ensure an increase in confidence and self-esteem.

HOW DO I PREVENT MY CHILDREN INHERITING MY LOW SELF-ESTEEM?

Regularly I am asked this question.

- Make sure children know they are loved, accepted and valued for who they are.
- Never criticise the child, only the behaviour.
- Discipline in a positive manner. They will never *learn* from being *told off.* They learn by example and explanation of the consequences of bad behaviour.
- Keep tone of voice calm and low.
- Never discipline out of anger. Wait until you calm down.
- Teach manners and the rules for becoming a responsible citizen.
- Show a child they are loved in spite of bad behaviour.
- Listen carefully to what they say.
- Give them time and encourage their opinions.
- Thank them when behaviour improves.
- Depending on age, you can ask why they behaved in a certain way.
- Regularly praise and encourage.
- Learn positive parenting skills.
- Lead by example.

Examples of phrases for disciplining:

- *We don't do that.*
- *Please stop, otherwise you will get hurt.*
- *That was an unkind thing to say, please apologise.*
- *Do you think that was a kind thing to do?*
- *Please share your toys.*
- *Please say sorry.*
- *What are the house rules regarding …*
- *Thank you for not …*
- *Thank you for stopping that.*

CORRECTING NEGATIVE SELF-TALK

Be aware of the language you use about yourself. Do you silently criticise yourself? Call yourself names?

Stop thinking and speaking negatively about yourself.

Note when you do this.

Ask a trusted friend or family member to prompt you if you are speaking negatively about yourself.

Some examples:

- *I am useless.*
- *I am so stupid.*
- *I never learn.*
- *I am an idiot.*
- *I am no good at ...*
- *I hate myself ...*
- *I am too fat, thin ...*
- *I always get it wrong.*
- *I am useless.*

Exercise

Note in your journal negative statements you use about yourself.

You can overwrite your negative self-talk with affirmations. Most of these statements begin with *I am*. The sub-conscious believes what you tell it. If you constantly tell it you are no good then it believes it. However, if you start to use positive statements about yourself, you will overwrite the negative self-talk. For this to be effective, you need to believe what you are telling yourself.

- *I am good enough.*
- *I like and approve of myself.*
- *I accept myself unconditionally.*
- *I am caring and kind.*
- *I learn from my mistakes.*
- *I am proud of who I am.*
- *I treat others with respect.*
- *I treat myself with respect.*
- *I walk with dignity.*
- *What others think of me is of no concern.*
- *As long as I approve of myself, others will follow.*

Remember: only use affirmations you believe. You cannot lie to the sub-conscious.

You could record/write some of these into your mobile phone to remind yourself, when you know you are thinking negatively about yourself.

SELF-ESTEEM & THE NEED TO BE LIKED

The need to be liked and approved of is a part of a low self-esteem. This need can be all consuming as it causes the fear of rejection. Dealing with fear of rejection is one of the top requested topics when a new course is started.

With a low self-esteem comes neediness and needy people will experience emotional difficulties in forming nurturing relationships. They may subconsciously be looking for what was absent in childhood. They have a need to be loved and accepted and will fear rejection. This need will drive their lives and the pursuit can cause much heartache.

By understanding and accepting that which happened in childhood was the result of those around them loving them in the only way they knew how, they can now see the problem was just a lack of parenting skills. By seeing this from a different perspective, accepting it and knowing that a healthy self-esteem can be acquired will be a massive step forward.

The past cannot be changed but it can be built on for a positive and enriching future.

Exercises

- Write a list of the qualities in the people you admire.

- Tick all the qualities from that list which you possess. (You could ask someone who knows you very well to help you.)

- Did you tick most of the same qualities? Friendships attract like for like. We are attracted to those with similar qualities.

When you become confident in your qualities and accept yourself for who you are, you will find others will follow and accept, not reject you. When people feel rejected through the actions of others it is because in some way they are actually rejecting themselves. When you accept yourself unconditionally, others will follow.

GOLDEN RULES FOR DEVELOPING A HEALTHY SELF-ESTEEM

- Patience. It will not happen overnight. It takes 21 days to form a new habit. (You will have relapses but this book will teach you how to cope with these.)
- Learn to let go of the past and live in the present moment.
- Let go of blaming others and self-blame.
- Keep a journal of your progress.
- Stop personalising.
- Silently praise and encourage yourself. This will replace any lack of praise and encouragement in earlier life.
- Use your name when you praise yourself. This act will also increase your self-confidence. *Well done (name)*. People with confidence sub-consciously do this, not exactly using those words but they know when a job is well done.
- Stop apologising for yourself.
- Mistakes are our best teachers. Look for the lesson learnt instead of chastising yourself.
- Stop being a perfectionist. Those with a low self-esteem tend to be extra hard on themselves seeking perfection in order to gain approval.
- Accept compliments graciously. It is a sign of a healthy self-esteem. When someone says something nice say *thank you*. A compliment is a gift. You wouldn't give back a gift so accept the compliment graciously and it will make the giver feel good too.
- Doing things for others increases self-esteem, thus showing the benefits of thinking outside of yourself.
- Never indulge in self-pity, it is self-destructive.
- Genuinely praise and encourage others.

Tick the qualities you possess.

Turn them into affirmations by adding I am ... and record them in your journal each evening until they become automatic thoughts.

- Kind
- Caring
- Thoughtful
- Generous
- Helpful
- Supportive
- Friendly
- Trustworthy
- Diligent
- Warm
- Loving
- Loyal
- Good fun
- Exciting
- Charismatic
- Interesting
- Sympathetic
- Dignified
- Likeable
- Approachable
- Non judgemental
- Fair
- Honest
- Reliable
- Hard working
- Compassionate
- Dependable
- Forgiving

This list was created by my students as the qualities they would most look for in others and would like to possess themselves.

You will be able to add more to the list.

Practise writing these as affirmations in your journal.

AM I A BAD PERSON?

I am frequently asked this question by students and when they explore their own qualities they discover they are far from a bad person. In most cases their qualities include them being:

- *Unselfish*
- *Loving*
- *Over-generous*
- *Kind*
- *Over-helpful*
- *Apologetic*
- *Over-considerate*

It is sad that they have this distorted view of themselves. The belief system may have come from childhood messages involving anger and manipulation. That belief system giving them a guilt complex in adulthood for which they will spend the rest of their lives over-compensating. In times of family arguments often all our bad points are thrown at us. Dwelling on these can lead to the belief of being a bad person.

We all do things we regret but that does not label us a bad person forever. In most situations where we feel we did not act in the right manner it was because we didn't know any different. Had we known better, we would have acted differently. Think back to anything you regret doing and ask yourself that question.

SELF-WORTH

When I ask students to define self-esteem, they will answer self-worth, however what does this mean?

One definition given:

How you see yourself; do you see yourself as worthless, worn down by criticism or confident and assertive?

We tend to assess ourselves through the criticism of others. It is a powerful tool in taking away confidence. Someone's critical voice can become your own. A voice which tells you that you are not good enough or do not measure up.

Are you carrying around someone's critical voice and using it as your own?

A student described how after divorcing a controlling and critical partner, thinking she would be free once they had parted, discovered that his critical voice lived on in her head for many years.

Exercise

- Keep a note of when you criticise yourself, note if it is your voice or someone else's critical voice.

- Change the language you are using. For example: *You idiot* becomes *never mind, it's not so bad, better luck next time.*

- Lighten up on your self-criticism, it will hold you back not spur you on to do better.

PROGRAMME FOR INCREASING SELF-ESTEEM

Aim to do at least three from the list each day.

- Genuinely praise others.
- Stop self-criticism.
- Learn self-praise.
- Be aware and live by your values because they define who you are. Never compromise on your values.
- Accept yourself.
- Be your own best friend. Unconditionally accept yourself.
- Small acts of kindness to others.
- Lighten up – laughter raises esteem.
- Keep a record of compliments.
- Stop personalising.
- Never act like a victim because victims never win.
- Stop blaming circumstances for how you are feeling.
- No self-pity as it is unattractive.
- Use affirmations to raise self-esteem.

Treat yourself. Do something just for you. (People with low self-esteem can find it difficult to treat themselves.) You are worth it.

SELF-PRAISE DAY

This was an exercise devised during a course for students who said they could never ever praise themselves. Students described how their confidence increased on the days they did this exercise.

- Book a date in your diary.

- For one day silently praise yourself, using your name throughout the day.

- After every action/task, even making the bed affirm to yourself *well done … name.*

Students have said this also increased their confidence levels and the way others reacted to them.

Old beliefs such as *self-praise is no recommendation* prevent acknowledging it when one has done something well. You need to know when you have succeeded. Confident people are aware of their successes.

WE ARE WHAT WE THINK

Having a low self-esteem means having a low opinion of yourself. You may have been taught that it is unattractive to have a high opinion of yourself, that it is vain and boastful. (The opposite is true. Quietly having a high respect and regard for yourself is important.)

Your thoughts affect your body language and your body language says more than the words you speak. If you have a low opinion of yourself it will show in your body language.

If internal dialogue is one of self-criticism this will be displayed in your body language and without realising it you will be inviting others to treat you the same way you treat yourself. That is why people with a low self-esteem attract bullies, not only are they low risk, but the bully confirms their worst thoughts.

Paul McKenna in his book *Instant Confidence* says that we are constantly telling others how to treat us by the way we treat ourselves.

If we change that critical internal voice to a loving caring voice, in time our body language will change and we will attract loving caring people into our lives.

People with a low self-esteem are usually loving and caring to others but not to themselves.

Exercise

Note in your journal what changes you need to make to your thought process in order to display confident body language.

PERSONALISING

Taking things personally is a sign of a low self-esteem.

People who take things personally are not seeing the bigger picture of what is happening because they are only focusing on their own view of a situation.

Is this you?

The way to obtaining a healthy self-esteem is to let go of personalising.

Personalising distorts thinking and damages relationships.

Never take anything personally, except a compliment.

The following is a list created by students as examples of what they take personally:

- Being passed over for promotion.
- Failing a job interview.
- End of a relationship.
- Being ignored.
- Someone forgetting their birthday.
- Phone calls/texts/emails not being returned.
- A date being cancelled.
- Being excluded.
- Bullying.

Instead of looking for logical reasons for the above they take the behaviour personally and fail to deal with it appropriately.

Think about situations where someone has taken something personally you have said or done and completely misinterpreted the situation. How did you feel?

This was the hardest task for students to master, but the most important as it can affect so much with confidence, self-esteem and assertiveness. It serves no positive purpose. It causes extreme distress.

People who take things personally are a pain. (It sounds harsh but it is true and that is why it needs to stop.)

Exercise

In your journal note all the times you take something personally. Write it down and then look for other reasons for the behaviour.

Example: A call not being returned. Could it be they have lost their phone or are busy, or just plain forgot?

It is important that personalising is dealt with early on in order to be more confident and assertive. More importantly to improve self-esteem.

The way to stop taking things personally is to practise seeing all sides of a situation. Next time you find yourself taking something personally, forget your own reaction and feelings and look at the situation from their side.

In your journal answer these questions:

- Was that an appropriate thing to say or do?

- What could have happened to make them act like that?

- What is going on in their life at the moment?

- How would someone outside of this situation view it from both sides?

- Now I have looked at this from different viewpoints, can I change the way I think and stop personalising?

- What have I learnt from this situation?

EVICT THE CRITIC THAT LIVES IN YOUR HEAD

Get rid of the critic that has lived in your head since childhood.

It has been there too long, always ready to tell you when you are not measuring up. It will appear when you least need it, without fail, when you have a difficult task to perform. It will tell you that you will not be able to do it.

You have been used to your critical voice for so long, you may be a little scared of being without it.

Affirmations are the first step in removing the critical voice, and replacing it with a more loving, encouraging voice.

Affirmations are powerful.

A few years ago I was teaching a group of men (recovering alcoholics) how to build confidence and self-esteem. When they all walked into the room for the second lesson I noticed someone I didn't recognise. During feedback at the beginning of the lesson this man said he had been using one affirmation *I am as good as anyone else* each day as he left his home and locked his front door. This one daily act had increased his confidence so much that I didn't recognise him at the second lesson. He said his feeling of self-worth was so low he didn't at first want to come to the sessions. His excitement at how his confidence had increased in one week had made a positive impact on his life.

Exercise

- Note when your critical voice is active.

- Replace it with affirmations. For example, *I will have a go*. (We learn from our mistakes.)

- You may wish to do what that student did and use affirmations at specific times of the day.

- You don't need that critical voice. Think how you can silence it.

- Keep a record of compliments and praise received.

- Regularly look at your CV to remind yourself of all you have achieved. A CV is an excellent record of all your achievements and positive qualities.

Some students write affirmations on Post It Notes and stick them in prominent places to remind them to think differently. One student wrote his on a card and read them whilst travelling by train to work.

This also works well with managing anxiety. Making yourself aware of all you can do.

Decide which affirmations you know to be true about yourself and which could improve your feeling of self-worth. Keep repeating them daily for 21 days.

STOP SAYING *SORRY*

Overuse of the word *sorry* is a sign of low self-esteem.

People don't know they are doing it. They preface statements with *I am sorry:*

> As they phone or ask a favour:
> *I am sorry to bother you.*
> *Sorry to be a nuisance.*

This is unnecessary. Just say what you need to say without saying *sorry* first.

> *Sorry I'm late.*
> *Instead,* use the word apologise *I apologise for being late.*

If you need to apologise then use the word *apologise*. It is more powerful than *sorry*.

By over-using the word *sorry* you are communicating that you are a people pleaser and have a lack of confidence with a low self-esteem. By over use of the word *sorry* you could open the way for others to take advantage or even bully.

It is not assertive to use the word *sorry*.

Some people feel it is polite to say *sorry*. If it is used in the correct context, then it is appropriate. For example; to a family member *I am sorry if I was inconsiderate*. However, bumping into someone in the street, use *apologise*. In everyday conversation *sorry* is not necessary.

Exercise

If you over use the word *sorry*, fine yourself each time you say it (50p) for 21 days.

Buy yourself a treat with all the money you have saved.

GUILT

Guilt is felt by those with a low self-esteem. How to remove the feeling of guilt is one of the most frequently requested topics.

Guilt is an emotion which is learnt in childhood (possibly feeling a sense of guilt following being disciplined). Giving a feeling of not measuring up to what is expected.

Guilt is a wasted emotion serving no purpose unless it is genuine and not habit. If you felt guilty because you were rude to someone then it is a prompt to apologise. However, most guilt is unnecessary. If you cannot make amends for your guilt, then let go of it.

Most people who experience guilt find the emotion is constantly with them when there is no evidence for feeling guilty.

Feeling guilty is another habit to break. People take advantage of those who suffer guilt. It invites manipulative behaviour.

Exercise

- When you next feel guilty, write in your journal what you are feeling guilty about.

- Is there any reason you need to feel guilty?

- Did you do the best you could in the situation?

- Was someone manipulating you/crossing your boundaries?

- Affirm *I am letting go of this feeling of guilt because I have done nothing wrong.*

(More about guilt and saying *no* in Assertiveness section.)

JEALOUSY

Jealousy can be an emotion felt by those with a low self-esteem. People can feel jealous of those around them who display the confidence they would like to possess.

Jealousy is self-destructive. It can cause people to bully others.

If you suffer from jealousy use the feeling as a prompt to check what you are not doing in your life which is causing you to feel like this.

Ask yourself what changes you can make to your life.

Example: if all your friends are getting married and you are not even dating then make plans to meet new people. If all around you are getting promotion at work and you feel stuck in your job, research gaining extra training to add to your qualifications.

Jealousy is self-destructive and needs to be addressed.

Positive action stops negative feelings.

If you are on the receiving end of the behaviour from a jealous person, see tips on how to manage it under the section on *Bullying*.

REJECTION

How to cope with rejection is at the top of requests from students. They ask how they can deal with the fear of rejection and rejection itself.

Rejection is how we choose to view a situation. Someone with a high sense of self-worth will not see the following situations as rejection, showing that we have a choice in how we view:

- Not getting a job we wanted.
- Being left by a partner.
- Not being picked for a school play.
- Not getting a second date.
- Being left out of a social circle.

These are some examples. The feeling of rejection may be that something in adulthood triggers an experience from childhood. It could have been parents divorcing, or a sibling being favoured more.

Fearing rejection shows in body language as being desperate. Being desperate is a turn off. Remove the word rejection from your vocabulary and thoughts. It is how you view the situation which is important. Look for alternative evidence:

Not getting a job just means someone else was more suited.

Being left by a partner could mean, the partner had the courage to leave a relationship that was not working.

Not being picked for the school play – a child needs reassurance here to ensure they do not see it as rejection. It is a good lesson to learn early in life.

Not getting a second date. There could be several reasons: they were seeing someone else already. They are not ready for a relationship. They could see it wasn't going to work for them.

Being left out of a social circle. It may just be an oversight. Stop dwelling and don't give it a second thought.

The pain of rejection may feel unbearable but it probably has more to do with triggering childhood memories and feelings than the current event.

Confident people who have a sense of self-worth will never see themselves as being rejected. They look for the lesson learned in every situation.

Learn from situations where you felt rejected. Be strong and move on.

FEAR OF REJECTION

There is the feeling of rejection and there is the fear of rejection. The fear of rejection can be worse than actual rejection. It can be all consuming. It can ruin relationships.

Fear is about something in the future which may or may not happen. It may be based on previous experiences. It is important to keep in mind the following:

- No two situations are the same.

- Just because something happened in the past it does not mean it will happen again.

- In your mind, face the worst that could happen and plan how you would deal with it if it did happen. When there is a plan in place, it is usually not needed.

- Live life in the present moment, rather than worrying what might happen. If you have a plan in place should the worst happen, you can put it to the back of your mind and stop worrying.

- Forget the word *rejection* and see a situation from all sides.

- If you fear rejection in a relationship, ask yourself what it is that you really fear. Is it the end of a fantastic relationship? Is it loss of face with your peers/family? Is it fear of being alone?

- The rejection you fear, should it occur, may not be anything to do with you. People and circumstances change. The job you wanted may have been withdrawn or given to someone working within the organisation.

Affirmations:

I can handle it if he/she doesn't call.
I can handle it if I don't get the job.
I can handle it if I don't get chosen for the team.

Or if you prefer:

I will handle it if they don't call.
I will handle it if I don't get the job.
I will handle if I don't get chosen.

Find what works for you.

Write the affirmations in your journal. Writing these new thoughts is a powerful way of learning to think in a positive manner.

Fear is about the future. Learn to live in the present moment.

REJECTION – ACCEPT, LET GO, MOVE ON

If the worst you fear does happen and a relationship comes to an end then grieve for the loss but only for a short time. Accepting, letting go and moving on is important.

Acceptance is the key to peace of mind.

The same with any form of loss. There has to be a suitable time to grieve for the loss but then moving on and building a new life is important.

Many of my students carry the pain of rejection for far too long after a relationship has ended. Although their former partner has a new life they are unable to let go and move on. In some cases the pain is made worse with a trigger from a childhood experience. Maybe a parent died or parents divorced.

At the end of a relationship, if you are unable to move on try to think what the other person might be doing while you are fretting over the loss of the relationship. They have moved on and presumably are enjoying life. Do you want to be miserable while they are having fun? Isn't that a powerful enough reason to learn to move on? If you look for lessons learnt it puts a positive focus on something which has devastated your life. You then need to start moving on with life and live it to the full.

You can take control of your feelings by telling yourself you certainly don't want to be with someone who doesn't want to be with you. Hold on to your dignity, it is important.

You need to let go of the past in order to make space for new experiences.

If it is still painful and difficult to do then seek professional help with a therapist. Cognitive Behaviour Therapy will help with moving on and give you new tools to use in the future.

Revenge never works. The best and only revenge that works is to pick yourself up, hold your head high and move on with dignity.

FORGIVENESS

A gift you give yourself.

People say *I can forgive but I can't forget.* That doesn't work if you truly want to be free and have peace of mind. You need to do both. Not forgiving and forgetting is like drinking poison and expecting the other person to die.

You don't have to forgive. It is not mandatory, but you do need to accept, let go, move on and forget.

To forgive means that you no longer carry any resentment for something someone did. The other person need never know you have forgiven them.

To forgive is freeing.

Forgiveness is a controversial subject but I have never seen a happy person who is unable to forgive. Not forgiving doesn't bring happiness.

For many, forgiveness does not enter into their thoughts, they just accept what someone did; learn from the situation and move on.

If forgiveness can be viewed as letting go of resentment and moving on, it may be easier to achieve.

Moving on from some situations may mean still being mindful of not falling victim to certain behaviours again.

Exercise

Try this exercise to see how it works for you.

Write down any resentment you are holding on to as not forgiving someone.

I forgive ... and release that person from my thoughts.

You should now feel more in control. If you want to feel even more in control try writing the following:

I forgive ... and release them from my thoughts, and to happiness.

Students have found this hard to do but worth the effort in the long term.

LETTING GO OF THE PAST

Letting go is an important part of a healthy self-esteem.

Any type of loss, especially bereavement, needs a time for grieving. However, one needs to be aware when it is time to move on. You may never get over the loss but you will in time get used to it and life will take on a new direction.

Are you holding on to anything from the past which you need to let go of? It is important to recognise if this is happening because it may be a major part of you moving forward. Mindfulness teaches about living in the present moment. It is important to live in the present moment. Mindfulness means living in the present, not fretting about the past or worrying about the future.

Symbolic gestures can help with letting go. Writing a letter expressing your feelings (but not EVER sending it). Releasing a balloon into the air, taking your past worries with it. These gestures give messages to the sub-conscious that you are moving on.

Exercise

Write a list of all you need to let go of in your life.

It is freeing to be able to say *I've let go of that.*

STOP BEING A VICTIM

Victims never win.

Children who have suffered any type of abuse may automatically grow up with a victim mentality without realising it. It is common that sufferers, whilst blaming others, will also take some of the blame themselves.

Blaming others puts you in victim mode and as victims never win, you need to work on moving from this mode into one of control.

If you are a victim you are not in control.

Being a victim links with personalising. By working on the exercises in this book to stop personalising you will be moving yourself from being a victim to being in control.

It is all right to feel cross or angry (remember to express anger appropriately so you are not controlled by the other person) at another's behaviour because it shows you have taken control. There is a difference between:

My father always put me down, bullied me, belittled me in front of others.

and

I feel angry that my father always put me down but I understand his background and now I don't take this personally. I was too young to understand and I know it was about him.

Please note: with serious forms of abuse whether mental or physical do seek professional help and don't try to battle it out alone.

Triggers in adult life may put you in victim mode for a while. You can tell if you are behaving as a victim, if you are blaming others. If you find yourself in victim mode, try the following:

- Take control by stopping blaming others.
- Take responsibility for your life and your recovery.
- Catch your victim thoughts, you will know what they are and how they start.
- Learn assertive responses to inappropriate behaviour.
- Deal with anger issues. Remember those who make you angry are controlling you.
- Look at your stress levels, if you are blaming those around you for how you feel, you may be stressed or overworked.
- A victim who blames others is powerless.
- A confident, assertive person recognises inappropriate behaviour and sees the situation from outside of their own perspective, then chooses how they will deal with it.
- When you feel upset at the way you have been treated, question your own feelings:
  o Am I reacting to feelings rather than facts?
  o Write down what has happened and see if you can look at the situation differently.
  o Has this situation triggered past memories and feelings which have nothing to do with the present situation?
- Use CBT (Cognitive Behaviour Therapy) to get a realistic and balanced view of the situation.
- Take responsibility for your reaction. That way it keeps you in control.
- Be more concerned with how you reacted than with what happened.
- Self-pity is destructive and separates feelings from facts.
- There are no benefits in being a victim.
- There are huge benefits in taking control.
- Friends get tired of helping someone who is always taking the victim route.
- Feel the benefits of not being a victim and list them in your journal. It will help the next time you get a trigger which sends you into victim mode.
- Take responsibility for your life.
- Forgiving removes you from victim mode and is freeing.
- When you hold a grudge or resentment about another person

you have created an emotional link which can become strong. You can break that link by forgiving their behaviour, accepting how they behave and moving on with your own life. It makes life much easier.

- Think outside of yourself. Do something for someone to make them feel better.
- Accept you will relapse. When this happens take a break. All this self-help can be exhausting.

A positive result of a bad experience is to emerge no longer a victim.

LETTING GO OF THE NEED TO BE LIKED

Like and approve of yourself and others will follow.

Being needy and wanting to be liked is not attractive. To illustrate this, I walked into my lecture room with a notice on my forehead *I WANT TO BE LIKED*. The students said it made them want to keep well away. I explained that needy people don't need a notice, their body language gives the same message.

Desperation is unattractive. Being self-assured and confident is attractive.

As long as you like and approve of yourself you don't need to worry whether people like you or not. Act as if they do, and if they don't there isn't much you can do about it. Most people are more worried about themselves so they are not thinking about or judging you. People are thinking about you a lot less than you realise.

If someone makes it obvious they don't like you, there is not a lot you can do about it. It may be they are jealous of you or you remind them of someone or they feel insecure. It is not worth the effort of trying to fathom out why. People with manners and integrity would not let their feelings show.

As long as you like and approve of yourself then others will follow.

ANXIETY

A feeling of dread, that something awful is going to happen.

There are varying degrees of anxiety. There are panic and anxiety disorders and then just general feelings of being anxious over quite minor things. If you think you have an anxiety/panic disorder you can seek professional help on how to manage it. It can overwhelm everything, if you allow it to take control.

Some people are born with an anxiety gene; it can be inherited. Others will suffer bouts of anxiety as a result of stress. If they have experienced a trauma, they may suffer a bout of anxiety.

It can be frightening suddenly to experience anxiety over events that others take in their daily stride. If you have a bad cold most people are sympathetic, however, if you say you are experiencing anxiety, most people will not understand. They think it is something you should be able to control. That it is why you need carefully to choose in whom you confide. There is no shame in anxiety; it is just that it is hard for those who have not suffered it, to understand.

Cognitive Behaviour Therapy is an excellent method for reducing anxious thoughts. You can do this with a therapist.

Here are some quick tips for managing anxiety.

Acceptance is the key to coping.

- Dwelling on anxiety and anxious thoughts makes it worse and will not cure it.
- Distracting from anxious thoughts has a positive effect.
- If you know you suffer from anxiety, put a plan in place for managing it as soon as you can.
- Exercise is good for reducing anxiety.
- Relaxation exercises help some people.
- Channel your anxiety so that you can get something positive out of it. For example: take up a new interest.

- Reading helps distract anxious thoughts.
- Breathing exercises.
- Meditation/one minute mediation.
- Make the hours between 9.00p.m. and 7.00a.m. a no worry zone. Get into the habit of being strict, so that you do not worry during these hours.
- Ensure you get 7-9 hours' sleep each night.
- Find someone in whom you can confide.
- Be prepared for others not to understand and do not let it affect you.
- Know when your anxious thoughts are at their worst and plan a distraction activity.
- Hunger and dehydration can make anxiety worse.

Acceptance doesn't mean you need to tell everyone, (unless you want to) it means you accept that at times you are anxious and there is nothing wrong with that.

When your brain realises you know how to manage anxiety, each bout should lessen in intensity.

Exercise

As soon as you start to feel anxious or you know there is an important event on the horizon, start your regime well in advance.

Give your anxiety level a score out of ten. Aim each day to reduce it by one. If your anxiety level is at 9 aim to get it to 8 and so on. By starting slowly to reduce it you are more likely to retain a lesser feeling of anxiety. Accept it may not go overnight.

- In your journal write all that you are grateful for that day. (This focuses the mind outside of the anxiety.)

- Plan your exercise routine. It could be short ten minute walks or more intense exercise.

- Build in some fun time. Watching a comedy film or meeting with friends who are lively company.

- Think of something you can do for others. This is one of the best things for reducing anxiety because you are thinking outside of yourself.

- Listen to music that inspires you.

- Check your diet; ensure it is healthy. You need to avoid too many carbohydrates, sugar (and alcohol).

- Give yourself worry time. Ten minutes per day, for example. Write worries on a sheet of paper and put away in an envelope till the next day. This helps you to stop dwelling.

- Seek out the company of others. It is not easy when you feel anxious but it will help to distract those thoughts.

- Write in your journal what works for you.

SOCIAL ANXIETY

Also known as social phobia.

Known as one of the most common anxiety disorders. It is a fear of social situations. It can be anything from shopping, speaking on the phone, going to parties and other social events. People fear starting conversations, meeting strangers, eating and drinking in public and talking to people in authority.

There is a fear of doing or saying something embarrassing. This fear is overwhelming. Some examples of causes:

- This could have started in childhood with over-protective parents who speak for their children.

- Constantly being criticised.

- Over emphasising stranger danger. Parents who themselves have social anxiety.

You can get professional help such as Cognitive Behaviour Therapy.

You could try self-help. Facing your fear is the first step to overcoming it:

- By doing the confidence and self-esteem exercises in this book.

- Starting with small steps. You could smile at someone you don't know or just say *hello*. (Only in a safe environment.)

- Walk into a room full of strangers knowing that you have an escape route should you need it.

- Decide to go to a party for half an hour. You can tell your host you are only able to look in for a short while. (You may find yourself staying a lot longer.)

- Students have told me this fear, in confidence, about coming into my class. We agree that they just stay for a short while and that they can leave the classroom for a break if they need it. By taking this relaxed approach, they have, in all cases, stayed for the whole session.

- If the fear is overwhelming you can try writing in your journal at the end of each day everything that has gone well in your day. This exercise moves you to thinking about something more positive. This helps to redress the balance if you are going through a stressful time.

To get a bout of social anxiety suddenly, which could include, travelling, fear of crowded places, lifts or the underground, it may be that you have gone through a series of stressful events one after another or all at the same time and this is a mechanism for keeping yourself safe. It should pass as the general stresses are overcome. If not, seek professional help.

FORGET THE BAD,
REMEMBER THE GOOD

It is common practice that those with a low self-esteem will remember word for word unkind comments people have made. People with a healthy self-esteem seldom remember unkind or hurtful comments because they instinctively know that just because someone says something, doesn't mean it is true.

Students will argue *why say something if it isn't true?* People play mind-games and it will be more about them than you. It can be a cover for their own inadequacies. Beware of the grain of truth when someone says something unkind. Don't dwell on what they have said. Feel compassion for them, they obviously have their own issues. The compassion will add to your own sense of integrity.

Learning the reasons why people do and say what they do is useful in understanding relationships.

Exercise

Keep a record of kind and complimentary things people say. This will help you to overwrite memories of unkind and hurtful comments.

PERFECTIONISM

Perfectionism is another indicator of a low self-esteem. The rationalisation is that by being perfect it should lead to acceptance; however, the opposite is true. Perfectionism causes much stress. Perfectionists set their own high standards, often higher than those set by others and nothing they ever do is good enough. Perfectionists are seldom successful because they wouldn't recognise success when they reached it.

Excellence (the best you can do/be) is achievable, perfection is not.

Some people would never admit to being a perfectionist because they know the psychological implications. Others are proud that they are perfectionists because they think it means they have high standards. Perfectionists suffer high degrees of stress, never achieving the perfection they crave.

Knowing that what you do is good enough and the best you can deliver, is all you need to do to achieve excellence.

Start telling yourself, *that's good enough*. Know when to let go and take the pressure off yourself. Know when you have done your best.

Artists are known for perfectionism; they learn when to let go of a painting otherwise they will ruin it. It is very seldom an artist will stand back from their work and say *I am pleased with that*.

Successful people are not perfectionists because they know perfection does not exist. They aim for and achieve excellence.

CONFIDENCE

Fake it till you make it

WHAT IS CONFIDENCE?

A positive feeling arising from an appreciation of one's own abilities. (OED).

Or simply translated, *I can do it.*

Lack of self-confidence usually starts in childhood, like low self-esteem. If you have a low opinion of yourself, it is difficult to be self-confident. One follows the other.

Confidence needs to be worked at. It means knowing what you can do rather than dwelling on what you can't do.

We all lack confidence in some areas. Building confidence is about knowing your strengths and playing to them.

Exercise

List all the things you can do, whether or not you consider you are good at them. Keep adding to the list. Add your transferable skills.

ENEMIES OF SELF-CONFIDENCE

- Low self-esteem.
- Self-doubt.
- Reluctance to *have a go*. (*If I can't do it perfectly, I'd rather not do it all.*)
- Fear of making mistakes.
- Negative thinking.
- Comparing yourself to others.
- Taking criticism personally.
- Stress.

Mistakes are our best teachers, as long as we learn from them. Entrepreneurs on average have one success to every seven failures. What makes them successful is that they never give up.

Never compare yourself to others. Observe and learn from others but never compare. You are unique, be confident in that.

Use criticism in a positive way. Evaluate it; if you think it is valid, learn from it, but don't confuse criticism with constructive feedback.

WHAT DOES CONFIDENCE MEAN TO YOU?

What could you do if you felt more confident?

How would your life improve if you had more confidence?

What is holding you back from being more confident?

Carefully think about those questions and write your answers in your journal.

Being more confident is not a measurable goal. Many people would like more confidence but are not specific in exactly what they would be able to do. For example: *with more confidence I would enrol on a language course. With more confidence I would join a social group.*

Exercise

Visualise yourself in six months' time with more confidence.

- How do you look?
- What are you doing?
- What are you saying?
- Where are you?
- Who is there with you?

Having this visualisation turns *being more confident* into a measurable goal.

What changes are you going to make now to work towards your own visualisation?

Example

Visualising yourself in a new job. By visualising yourself in the role, it will help you to reach the goal because you have a picture which you can work towards. It will not just happen; you need to make it happen. That is confidence. Successful people picture their success and work towards it; it doesn't happen by accident. Success follows hard work. But first you need a dream to work towards.

When teaching public speaking, I get students firstly to picture themselves giving a successful speech and the audience's positive reaction. This gives them a goal to work towards. Then the hard work begins to achieve that dream.

FIND A ROLE MODEL

Choose someone you admire for their confidence. Identify what it is that makes them appear confident and self-assured.

Make a list of their qualities, for example:

- Appearance – smart and well-groomed.
- Posture.
- Well organised.
- Self-assured.
- Calm.
- Stress-free.
- Tone of voice.
- Positive body language.
- Sense of humour.
- Laid back/easy going.
- Assertive.
- Good listener.
- Healthy self-esteem.
- Interested in others.
- Self-reliant.
- Not self-absorbed.

Add more to the list if you can.

How can you acquire those qualities?

Make notes in your journal on how you will achieve some of those qualities.

TODAY I AM AIMING FOR EXCELLENCE IN ALL I DO

A tried and tested way to start your day with confidence.

Excellence is achievable. It simply means the best you can do/be. Do not confuse confidence with being perfect as explained in the previous section under self-esteem.

By starting the day with the following affirmation,

Today I am aiming for excellence in all that I do

you are programming yourself, in whatever you do, to do it with confidence.

By programming yourself for excellence, you are more likely to exceed your own expectations.

WHAT IF I COME ACROSS AS TOO SELF-CONFIDENT?

Or, worse, as big-headed. (I get asked this all the time).

As children we may have been raised with the belief that being over confident is bad. Anyone who fears this will never be over-confident because of the fact they fear it.

Self-confidence comes from within. Over-confident people are often hiding a low self-confidence. If you follow the exercises in this book, you will appear quietly self-assured and not over confident.

Confidence is not controlling, over-powering, or aggressive.

As long as you are not displaying any of those traits, then you will not appear over-confident; just quietly confident which is attractive.

FEAR

Fear is the main enemy of confidence and assertiveness.

- Fears diminish once confronted.
- Avoidance strengthens fear.
- Fear is the flipside of excitement. The feelings are similar.
- Excitement is what you will experience when you face your fears.
- Fear can warn of danger and that is when you need to listen to that warning.
- Fear of non-dangerous situations needs to be addressed.
- Fear of the fear. (Fearing the feelings of fear moves into the areas of phobias and anxiety and may need professional help.)
- Fear is future based. People fear something which may or may not happen.
- Fear of failure prevents people from fulfilling their potential.
- Failure is part of success and needs to be experienced in order to grow.
- With many fears you need to look at the situation, ask yourself even if it may be possible, is it probable?

The number one fear is public speaking. I know because I teach public speaking. Students who enrol on courses are confronting a major fear. It is an irrational fear because there is no physical danger connected to public speaking. Only feelings of danger. They are learning how to manage the anxious feelings associated with public speaking. By learning how to speak in public, a skill which needs learning, they overcome their worst fear.

A way to manage fear is to imagine the worst that could happen and how you would deal with it. Then put the fear aside.

Most fears involve making a fool of oneself; worrying about what others will think. In reality people are so busy with their own thoughts that they are not thinking about you at all.

Mindfulness is a great help in reducing fear. Mindfulness will teach you how to live life in the present moment.

There are many books on Mindfulness, find one which is written in a style you can follow.

When feeling fearful try a one-minute meditation (there are many you can use on YouTube).

FEAR OF FAILURE

Better to try and fail, than never to have tried at all.
Poem by William F O'Brien

To grow in confidence, you need to get rid of the fear of failure. You are a success because you tried.

Decide on a scale of 1-10 how severe this fear is. Anything over four will be affecting your confidence.

Fear of failure prevents you from having a go. If you are not failing at something in life you are not fully living. I fail miserably at gardening but that doesn't stop me each year having a go. Subsequently I have found what I can do, and that is instant gardening in pots. My garden now is frequently admired; not bad for a failure.

Many successful people have experienced a lot of failure in order to achieve their success. They are not afraid of failure. Failure has taught them what they need to do the next time.

Failure is part of success.

Exercise

- Write down something you feel you have failed at.

- Now list all the lessons you learnt from that failure.

- How would you do things differently next time?

If you fail an exam, look at all the knowledge you gained from studying for that exam. Most times you get the chance to re-sit an exam. Failure is giving up; success is having another go. However, this needs to be put into perspective: it is always good to know when to give up. If it is a conscious decision, fine, however you need to be sure you are not giving up because you fear failure.

FEAR OF MAKING A MISTAKE

Mistakes are the best teachers (as long as we learn from them).

This is a common fear and when under stress at work this fear can be overwhelming. Fear of making a mistake will prevent you from confidently succeeding at your work. It could be a signal that you need to take a break.

The more we fear making a mistake the more likely we are to make one. It will also use up a lot of emotional energy. Fear drains energy. Fear also prevents creativity. Tasks completed through fear, lack spontaneity and flow. One can feel paralysed through fear of making a mistake.

If you fear making mistakes, ask yourself *what is the worst that could happen?* Then put a plan in place should the worst happen. Most times you will not need your plan, but at least you have it; that should then give you peace of mind and freedom from worry.

Intelligence is learning from our mistakes.

PLAN FOR SUCCESS

Success breeds success.

The feeling of being successful is a powerful part of confidence. Success is the feeling of achievement you get from completing a task (however big or small) to the best of your ability.

Success is not just fame, money and position.

Make it a habit to work towards the feeling of fulfilment through achievement and you will become successful in all that you do. That feeling of success will do wonders for your confidence.

Start small. Complete small achievable tasks and praise yourself as you complete each task. A simple *well done* followed by your name.

Successful people set themselves up to succeed and that will mean failing sometimes. They learn from their failures and come back stronger with the next attempt. There is excitement in setting yourself up to succeed.

Exercise

- Close your eyes and remember a time when you felt successful.
- What did you do to feel that way?
- Each night in your journal write your achievements for that day.

ANXIETY & CONFIDENCE

Anxiety attacks confidence.

Anxiety is a feeling of concern/worry/unease/fear about something where you are not certain of the outcome.

If you know you suffer from anxiety, make a plan to manage it so that it doesn't affect your confidence.

Think about how your anxiety manifests itself; here are some hints:

- You feel nervous about a situation.
- You fear what might happen.
- Shaking.
- Over-breathing.
- Feeling faint.
- Nausea.
- Sweating.
- Frequent visits to the toilet.
- A feeling of dread.

Exercise

Try the following before you really need it and see what works for you:

- Relaxation CD.
- Breathing exercises.
- Meditation.
- Drinking enough water to keep hydrated.
- Healthy eating.
- Exercise such as walking which is excellent for anxiety as it releases endorphins into the brain.
- Distract anxious thoughts.
- Stop dwelling on what might happen.
- One of the best immediate cures for anxiety is a brisk walk.
- *One-Moment Meditation* by Martin Boroson can be found online.

- If anxiety is severe seek professional help through your GP. Cognitive Behaviour Therapy can help with anxiety.

If you have always been an anxious person, accept your anxiety as part of who you are. By accepting it you will in time reduce the anxiety. Look for the plus side of anxiety. People with anxiety are sedom late for meetings and interviews. They plan ahead in order to avoid anxiety.

DEPRESSION/LOW MOOD

Depression takes away confidence. If you suffer from a low mood for longer than two weeks, see your GP.

Easy Ways to Lift Your Mood by Jennie Willett and Dr Peter Connell is a book designed to manage depression and low mood, with or without medication. The exercises in the book are designed to put the reader in control of their depression.

There are different forms of depression. One form of depression, possibly through burn-out can be a signal that life is telling you that you need to make changes. Don't make any major changes until you feel better as you may not be thinking clearly.

If a normally confident person suffers from low mood, they know it will pass and are confident in the fact that it will pass.

Whilst recovering look at mindfulness and possibly Cognitive Behaviour Therapy as a way of managing negative thinking.

STRESS

If you are stressed your confidence levels will drop. It is important, especially if you are working, to learn to manage your stress and ensure your confidence levels do not suffer.

Stress is a feeling of being overwhelmed, of not being able to cope and not being in control.

When you feel stressed give each situation a mark out of ten. You can write this in your journal. Anything over seven, ask yourself if it is worth getting stressed about. Stress can become a habit. If you miss a train you may feel frustrated because you will be late and give your stress a nine when in fact it is only a two. Many people with stress benefit from time management training.

Exercise

- 7-9 hours' sleep a night.
- Drink enough water/keep hydrated.
- Eat a healthy diet, low in salt and sugar.
- Avoid alcohol and sugary snacks. These are only quick fixes which are no good long term.
- Exercise regularly.
- Correct balance of work and play.
- Absorbing interests.
- Fun.
- Seeking out humour in everyday situations.
- Regular breaks.
- Not taking yourself too seriously.
- Know what causes you stress and take early action.

NEGATIVE THINKING

Negative thinking can be habit. Work on the exercises below to challenge your negative thinking. It takes 21 days to form a new habit. If you know you tend to think negatively about most things it will show in your body language, vocabulary and confidence.

Exercise

- The first step is to note when you are thinking negatively.
- Write down your negative thoughts.
- Look for evidence for thinking the way you do.
- Just because something bad happened in the past, it does not mean it will happen again, or if it does it will be different the next time.
- Every problem has a solution and you need to believe this.
- What changes do you need to make to overcome negative thinking?
- You cannot just change a negative thought to a positive thought. You need fully to believe your positive thinking.
- Look at a problem as an opportunity to grow.
- Ask yourself these questions:
  Do I really need to think this way?
  Is thinking this way helping me at all?
  How would I advise a friend if they were thinking this way?

Confident people use positive language. Ensure your negative thoughts don't become your negative vocabulary.

Don't be an habitual moaner groaner. It doesn't show confidence. Moaning can be therapeutic, occasionally. Check if you constantly moan and groan and make a conscious effort to stop.

WALK WITH CONFIDENCE

You will feel confident if you look confident. The way you dress and being well groomed is important for your self-confidence, especially in the workplace.

Look at how confident people walk; they look up, not down. The way they walk tells you how confident they are. You can always tell people with low self-esteem and low-confidence by the way they walk, shoulders hunched, looking downwards.

Your body language says more about you than the words you speak. Walking with confidence into an interview gives a good first impression. It is not something you can acquire overnight; it needs practice. Fake it till you make it.

If you are thinking confidently then your body language will be confident.

DAILY BONUSES

Our lives are a mixture of good and not so good things. Confident people focus on the good and not on the bad. If you are someone who dwells on the bad things in life start to look for bonuses each day.

Bonuses are pleasant surprises. Write them down so you focus on them more than negative things.

Looking for bonuses each day helps you to change from a negative to a positive outlook.

Each night write all the day's bonuses in your journal. Here are some examples:

- A beautiful day.
- Someone smiles at you.
- A kindness from someone.
- A compliment.
- Praise.
- Positive feedback on your work.
- An unexpected email/text from a friend.
- Finding a parking place.
- Getting a seat on the Tube.
- A present.

Make it a task to search for as many as possible each day.

ASSERTIVENESS

Communicating your needs through clear, honest dialogue.

Setting and maintaining boundaries.

WHAT IS ASSERTIVENESS?

Assertiveness is behaviour which is neither aggressive nor passive. It is firm and polite and relies on confidence and a healthy self-esteem. It is behaviour which sets and maintains boundaries and uses clear honest dialogue. Assertive people know their own rights and are sensitive to the rights of others.

Assertive people communicate on an equal basis; they do not have the need to control others or be controlled. They are confident in their own abilities and they know how to say *no* to anything they do not want to do, without feeling guilty. They are comfortable in admitting if they do not know something or are in the wrong. They do not have a problem apologising if they are in the wrong.

Fear, anger and guilt have no part in assertiveness. You cannot be assertive if you are fearful, angry or suffer from guilt. Assertive people do not have a fear of confrontation; they may not like it but they do not fear it.

Some students are concerned that others will not like them if they become assertive. Family and friends may at first find it difficult to accept the change in behaviour but in time it will earn respect.

Assertiveness earns respect because boundaries are created and people know where they stand.

BASIC PERSONAL RIGHTS

In class we separate into groups where each group draws up a list of *rights*. These are some of the most popular.

I have the right to:

- Happiness.
- Respect
- Not be bullied.
- Say *no*.
- Make mistakes.
- Be listened to.
- Be able to state my opinion.
- Live the life I choose.
- Be treated fairly.
- Be me.

Exercise

Write a list of your own basic personal rights:

I have the right to …

Then you can learn how to ensure your rights are respected.

SAYING *NO*

Saying no creates boundaries.

For a great many people saying *no* to unreasonable requests is difficult for a variety of reasons:

- *I want to be liked.*
- *I am afraid of the outcome.*
- *I don't want to be thought unhelpful.*
- *I don't want to feel guilty.*
- *It is easier to say yes.*
- *I don't want to explain myself.*
- *It seems rude.*

The reverse is true. Saying *no* earns respect. It stops you doing something you don't want to do. It creates clear boundaries.

Tone of voice is important. Lower your voice, keep calm.

Practise saying *no* until you are confident.*

You need to be sure it is appropriate to say *no*. At work or at school it may not be appropriate to people in authority.

* This is the main reason most people attend assertiveness courses.

HOW TO SAY *NO* AND NOT FEEL GUILTY

Say *no* without justifying and defending yourself. Justifying and defending will weaken what you are saying.

Tone of voice is more important than the actual words you speak. Keep a calm lower tone of voice.

Less is more. Don't weaken your argument by saying too much, or be afraid of silence during a conversation.

Using the other person's name strengthens what you are saying.

Here are some examples of assertive phrases:

No (name) I can't.
No (name) on this occasion I am unable to help.
No (name) I wish I could but I can't.
No (name) I can't help you, is there anyone else who can?
No (name) that is something I cannot do.
No (name) I can't this time but do ask me again.

The other person needs to hear the word *no*.

If you feel more comfortable apologising, then use the word *apologise*. Never use *sorry*.

It has to be appropriate to use the word *no*. At work, in certain circumstances, it may not be appropriate. It has to be your decision

Do not be afraid to use the word *no* if it is something you cannot do or do not want to do. You may feel guilty at first but you need to push through this fear of saying *no*.

Learn to create boundaries by using the word *no*. It shows that you respect yourself and know your boundaries. This is especially important in new relationships. Many relationships get into difficulties because clear boundaries were not set at the beginning.

SETTING AND MAINTAINING BOUNDARIES

It is important to know your boundaries and maintain them. You will know if someone has crossed your boundary because you will feel uncomfortable. Obey that feeling, it is a warning.

Our boundaries are influenced by our values and in order to be confident and assertive we never compromise our values because they define who we are.

Examples of crossing boundaries:

- Not taking *no* for an answer.
- Making rude comments.
- Showing lack of consideration.
- Physical/mental abuse.
- Bullying.

Confident assertive behaviour shows that you know your boundaries and will protect them. This is achieved through clear, honest dialogue without fear. Ensuring your safety is maintained.

Be confident in knowing and maintaining your boundaries.

NEVER DEFEND OR JUSTIFY YOURSELF
(*except in a court of law*)

A sign of non-assertive behaviour is needing to justify/defend what you say and do. Except in court, there is no need to defend or justify yourself.

Manipulative people use the technique of asking *why* you did or said something, then you have to justify, forcing you to give an explanation which can then be open to criticism. Learn to ask a question back; for example:

Q *Why do you always …?*

A *I'm interested why you have asked that.*

Recognise if you defend or justify yourself. This behaviour is saying that you want to be liked and should the other person agree or not agree with what you are saying/doing, then you have explained yourself, when in fact you are leaving yourself open to criticism.

Be confident in what you do and say and do not feel the need to explain yourself.

There are times at work where you may have to justify your actions and you will recognise when this is appropriate.

MANAGING DIFFICULT BEHAVIOUR

This is any behaviour you find difficult to deal with. This is one of the most requested topics on whatever subject I am teaching. It is one of the major causes of stress in the workplace.

Employers look for employees with good interpersonal skills, therefore learning how to manage difficult behaviour is important. It avoids complaints about bullying in the workplace which are seldom settled satisfactorily to all parties.

Behaviour *nipped in the bud* saves time and emotional distress. It deals with bullying before it takes a hold.

This is a list of behaviour students find difficult to manage. (Tick those which apply to you.)

- Bullying
- Criticism
- Rudeness
- Aggression
- Negativity
- Assertiveness
- Manipulation
- Racism, sexism, ageism
- Lack of respect
- Anger
- Patronising
- Jealousy
- Selfishness
- Control
- Belittling
- Sarcasm.

You may wish to add more of your own. Bullying always tops the list but it is easier to manage/report if the actual behaviour is identified and not given the global term *bullying*.

Identifying behaviour is the first step in managing it. Several of the exercises in this book need to come into action when dealing with difficult behaviour:

- Not personalising.
- Creating boundaries.
- Using clear, honest dialogue.

All difficult behaviour needs to be *nipped in the bud*. If not, it becomes difficult to manage.

Identifying the reasons why people behave the way they do is important. Becoming a victim is to be avoided at all costs because victims never win.

Bullies are weak and insecure and make themselves feel better for a split second if they can make another person feel scared or uncomfortable. They will target low risk people who are not likely to fight back. If you were bullied as a child you may find it more difficult to deal with bullies in adulthood.

If bullying has taken a hold, seek professional advice on how to manage it. It may be preferable to seek that help outside of your organisation. There is plenty of help online.

How you report bullying has a direct effect on the level of help you receive. If you can identify the behaviour and report bullying in a calm (not emotional) manner, assertively, you are more likely to receive the help you need.

Keep a record in your diary of incidents. (You may prefer to keep a separate diary at home for this purpose). It will look professional if you need to back up a complaint.

Many people in authority find it hard to respond to complaints of bullying. This is true also of many schools. They may display posters *WE DO NOT TOLERATE BULLYING* but in reality children and parents regularly fail to get the support and outcome they need. Bullying has always occurred in schools and always will, however it needs to be addressed both for the sake of the bully and the victim.

It is easier to discipline a child for specific bad behaviour rather than the global term of bullying.

If you suffered bullying as a child at school, you may overreact to bullying at work. The emotions you experienced as a child will be triggered as an adult. These reactions may be intense and others will not understand the reaction, that is why it is important to seek outside help and advice.

Bullying is relentless. Bullies target a victim. They can be perfectly nice to everyone else making their victim feel even worse and feel there is something wrong with them to have invited the bullying. With the cases of bullying I deal with in my private practice, the common factor is jealousy. I see smart, professional people, good at what they do who are often perceived to be a threat. The bully will look for a weakness and play on it.

The behaviour needs to be fairly constant to warrant the term bullying:

- Are you being targeted on a regular basis?
- Do you feel intimidated and unable to defend yourself?
- What do you fear?
- What effect is it having on your performance?
- What effect is it having on your health?

Here are some methods for dealing with difficult behaviour so that it does not turn into bullying. No two situations are the same so this is generic and not specific. Your safety has to come first. This is a brief overview.

- If you do decide to report it, be prepared to accept that the outcome may not be exactly what you would like. Before reporting have some idea of what you would like to happen. Do you want the person to be warned, or do you expect them to be disciplined or dismissed?

  People can suffer even more stress from not getting the outcome they wanted, than the stress they were getting from the bullying.

  The main outcome should be for it to stop.

- If it is overt, threatening behaviour which breaks the law, then you should have no problem in reporting.

Setting boundaries at work so that it does not turn into bullying will certainly make life easier and give you more confidence.

CRITICISM

No criticism is constructive. Positive feedback on how to improve is constructive. If you feel you are being overly and regularly criticised, you have choices, for example:

Ignore if it is rude and unkind.
Ask a question:
> *Thank you for the feedback, can you be more specific?*
> *I am not sure exactly what you mean, can you expand on that?*

Feedback key words: Example:
What you have just said is rubbish
Please can you tell me in what way it is rubbish?

Some confident people are fine with criticism and do learn from it. They don't take it personally and understand that there are people who don't know how to give feedback. They know how to view criticism, how to decide whether it is valid or not.

Responding in an assertive manner rather than reacting will gain you respect.

Many people would rather someone criticised them to their face than behind their back, managers for example. That way something can be put right earlier before it is an issue.

Key points in dealing with criticism:

1. Is it valid?
2. Can I learn from it?
3. Is it hurtful and unkind? Can I ignore it?
4. If appropriate ask a question to clarify what is being said.
5. Thank the person for bringing it to your attention.
6. Never take it personally, even if it may seem personal.
7. Some people are naturally critical; it is a form of bullying because they are unhappy in themselves.

You have choices on how you respond to criticism which gives you more control than you may think you have.

RUDENESS

Some people appear rude because that is their natural behaviour. Not everyone has had the advantage of being raised with consideration for the feelings of others.

Create boundaries which show that you disapprove of rudeness. Know when to it is safer not to take the matter any further and walk away. Know when you need to stand up for yourself.

Feeling sorry for someone who is rude is often the best way of dealing with it. Feel sorry because they have not been taught manners.

Never continue a conversation if someone is rude to you because that is giving them permission to continue. You could say, *I prefer not to discuss this further, thank you.* You will have created a boundary.

With general rudeness, by letting a person's comment *hang in the air* will allow the focus to remain on them, rather than you if you entered into an argument. Saying nothing can be extremely powerful.

If someone is rude try the following:

Pause – lower your voice – *excuse me?* This gives the other party time to correct their behaviour without confrontation.

Rudeness comes in so many forms it is impossible to cover every eventuality but once you learn assertive responses you will become confident in managing rudeness.

ANGER/AGGRESSION

Never try to reason with an angry person because they can't hear.

Give them time to calm down or walk away. (Your safety comes first.)

Acknowledge their anger:
I can see that you are angry about this; could we discuss it later?

Never react in anger. Nothing will be achieved.

NEGATIVITY

This is a regular topic in class. *How can I deal with negative people?*

The answer is that you cannot change a negative person into a positive one. It is their right to be negative.

You could discuss why they feel the way they do.

Here are some responses:

- *What is the outcome you would like?*
- *I see this in a different way.*
- *I am interested why you say that?*
- *Is there a way we can improve things?*
- *You may be right, but shall we give a try anyway?*

It can be easier to agree with a negative comment: *You may be right.*

Negativity is contagious so it is best to keep your distance, especially in the workplace. Stand back from the *moan and groan society*. It never achieves anything positive. Some people enjoy a moan and a groan and that is their right. It is also your right not to take part.

ASSERTIVENESS

You may wonder why I am including this under difficult behaviour when the book is mainly about assertiveness. Many people feel intimidated by assertive behaviour because it is honest and direct. Once they get used to communicating with assertive people and they themselves become assertive, it becomes less of a problem.

When you have learnt assertive dialogue/phrases and can communicate on an equal basis, you will gain more confidence.

Assertive people say what they mean, without emotion. They are direct and expect you to respond in the same manner. It may seem abrupt but it saves time and avoids misinterpretation. Their conversation as well as the written word (emails in the workplace) are direct and to the point without waffle.

Do not confuse assertiveness with rudeness or aggression. Assertive dialogue is polite and to the point, especially in the workplace.

Always be professional in the workplace. Assertive people are professional (for example: no kisses on emails!!!)

It is easier to communicate with an assertive person because you know where you stand.

MANIPULATION

This is difficult to manage because it involves mind games. People play mind games in order to gain control.

It is important to create boundaries with people who play mind games. They are doing this to get what they want. Never get involved in mind games.

Learn to trust your gut instinct. If you are talking to someone and you feel uncomfortable, take time to respond. Take a deep breath, and respond in an assertive manner.

Listen more than you speak.

- *I am not sure where this conversation is going. I need to think this through.*
- *I am not totally sure what you mean?*
- *Have I understood this correctly?*
- *I will need to get back to you on this.*
- *Give me time to think this through.*

RACISM

Racism is against the law. It can be reported and is taken seriously. Depending on the severity, you have the choice whether you take it further or not. Do not take it personally; this is how some people behave. It is ignorance.

Remember you are in control, you have the choice whether or not to report sexism, ageism, homophobia.

You have a choice whether to ignore or take the matter further. It can sometimes be more stressful to report.

In all cases seek professional advice and then make the choice of whether to report, depending on the severity.

LACK OF RESPECT

Unless you are in a position of authority it is difficult to define and demand respect. You cannot change disrespectful behaviour but you can change your reaction to it. Ignoring can be a powerful reaction, depending on the situation.

What one person sees as lack of respect another will view as ignorance and choose to ignore it.

This topic regularly comes up in class and it is difficult to define what students mean by it. It is probably covered under other types of difficult behaviour but they feel so strongly that I have decided to include it.

As long as you have respect for yourself and treat others with respect, using clear honest dialogue on an equal basis, you will grow in confidence and may find more respect is returned.

PATRONISING BEHAVIOUR

It is only patronising if you have a low self-esteem and view comments as patronising. With increased self-esteem and confidence, together with the use of assertive dialogue, responding to patronising behaviour becomes easier.

You have a choice.

To say nothing can be a powerful response.

If you do not view it as patronising, then the other party has lost control.

People who intentionally patronise feel insecure.

JEALOUSY

This is one of the main reasons bullying occurs. I see many clients who are victims of bullying in the workplace. Sometimes it is so subtle no-one else knows it is happening; other times it is overt and causes even more embarrassment to the victim.

Most times it is directed towards attractive/smart, intelligent, conscientious work colleagues. (The same in other organisations such as school/college/social situations.)

It manifests itself in many types of behaviour.

Learn to recognise jealousy. If you have a low self-esteem you cannot imagine why someone would be jealous of you, but trust me, I see enough cases to know the signs, however, I need the student to see it for themselves in order that we can move forward in dealing with it. Once the student recognises it is born out of jealousy they gain confidence.

Jealousy can be like an illness. Some people are consumed by jealousy.

Assertive responses, creating boundaries, moving away from the behaviour, are all ways of managing it.

The most important aspect for yourself is not to take it personally. Feel sorry for the other person but do not allow them to make your life a misery. If you are being bullied, tell someone you trust, whatever your age.

When people are unhappy with their own lives, they find it difficult to see others who are happy and successful.

Jealousy ruins lives. By identifying the behaviour will give you more insight on how to deal with it.

SELFISHNESS

Difficult to accept when people are only thinking of *number one* and appear to have no thought for others. You cannot change a selfish person's behaviour. You can change your reaction to it and ensure in an assertive manner it does not impinge on your own wellbeing.

- Create boundaries.
- Ensure your own needs are met.
- Use assertive dialogue.

A student gave an example how they were given a warning about someone they were going to work for. *They will always do what is right for them.* That was a delicate way of saying this particular person was selfish. That is a clear definition of selfishness and that powerful statement gave prior warning. In the long term people who behave in a selfish manner are not happy.

Their perceived success is only transitory.

The happiest people are those who are unselfish, considerate and give to others.

CONTROLLING BEHAVIOUR (BULLYING)

Depending on the severity decide whether you need to seek professional help.

It can be hard to break the pattern of controlling behaviour if it has taken a hold.

Mental abuse is more difficult to report than physical, however now it is gradually becoming easier.

People who control others are insecure and there are some similarities between the make-up of a bully and a victim.

Get help in moving from victim status. It is important to no longer be a victim. You have the right to lead a life free of control by others. Contact organisations such as Victim Support/Samaritans. Request anonymity but do seek professional help. Find helplines for your particular case.

People who recover from being a victim usually emerge stronger for the experience.

It is important to recognise that bullying behaviour, although it may seem like it, is not personal. If it wasn't you, they would find someone else. A bully needs a victim, it doesn't matter who it is, they just need someone to make them feel better through their controlling behaviour.

A victim will never forget who has bullied them. Bullies will, in most cases, never remember those they have bullied.

SARCASM

I was only joking.

Beware of that comment, someone may have ridiculed you and they then follow it with *I was only joking.* If it was a genuine mistake, they would apologise if their joke was taken the wrong way.

No reaction is the best reaction to sarcasm. Let their comment hang in the air so they feel embarrassed.

You can respond with *excuse me?* which delivered in a calm voice gives the other person time to correct their behaviour and avoids confrontation. It gives them the opportunity to rephrase what they have said in a polite form.

When a man points a finger at someone else, he should remember that four of his fingers are pointing at himself. Louis Nizer (lawyer).

WIN/WIN

In every situation aim for win/win. This is not about revenge or forgiveness. It is about making life as nice as possible for you and those around you. Notice if the past is getting in the way of the present. What would win/win mean to you?

- Is it a family get-together without an argument?
- A pleasant two-way conversation?
- A conversation without you being left feeling guilty?
- A meeting where you feel calm and in control?
- Being able to say when something is bothering you?
- Not being afraid to say *no* to an unreasonable request?
- You not experiencing any inappropriate reaction?
- Reducing tension and stress?

DON'T BE A VICTIM

Victims never win. Let go of being a victim, however bad the other person has behaved. When telling others, talk in facts and not as a victim. Use phrases like 'unacceptable behaviour'. Give the facts without the emotion. A close friend or counsellor may be able to help with the emotions but keep facts and emotions separate. Know to whom you can express your inner feelings without being judged.

LET GO OF THE PAST

Most family difficulties are based on the past. You cannot change the past, but you can learn from it. You may wish you had behaved differently but you cannot change the past. Make the next time you see that difficult family member a new beginning. (That does not mean being over-friendly or expecting immediate healing.) Like respect, healing needs to be earned. Until you are confident the relationship is more solid, be detached in order to protect yourself from getting hurt. Start afresh. The other party does not need to know. Lead by example. It is empowering.

However bad the behaviour has been in the past, try to let go of it and move on. In families this is important. It does not mean you accept or condone the behaviour, it means you are prepared to find a common ground on which to move forward.

ACCEPTANCE

Acceptance is the most important and hardest part of managing family difficulties. Accept the people for who they are. You cannot change them or hope they will change. They may not have the same values as you have and you need to accept that. You choose your friends but you can't choose your family. Accept them but do not allow them to behave inappropriately; you will need to set boundaries. Let go of the emotional link that causes you pain.

LET GO OF CONTROL

When in a difficult situation, especially with a family member, it is usual to try to retain some control. If you stop trying to hold on to control and let go (without allowing anything inappropriate to take place) you will become more relaxed. The more control you let go of, the more self-control you will end up with. Which means, by letting go of control, the other person is free to be themselves and situations are less tense. If anything offensive or inappropriate occurs then you need to employ assertive behaviour and set boundaries, or remove yourself from the situation.

DIFFICULT EMAILS/TEXTS

- Don't respond immediately.
- Think about your response.
- Read it out loud. How does it sound?
- Will it create a boundary?
- Will you achieve win/win?

TAKE ISSUE WITH THE BEHAVIOUR, NOT THE PERSON

If you need to set boundaries, refer to the behaviour, not the person. Separate the two. With children and adults alike, criticise the behaviour not the person.

Avoid 'you are …'

Use for example *that behaviour is unacceptable/inappropriate/ hurtful.*

USE I STATEMENTS

I statements are powerful. Learn how to use them.

I feel upset by what you said.

I feel hurt by your behaviour.

I don't know if I have understood this correctly but ...

I need some help in understanding your behaviour.

These I statements give the other party a chance to explain. Keep anger out of the discussion.

REMAIN CALM

Remaining calm is important, however angry you feel.

ANGER SOLVES NOTHING

You may want to bring up the past and tell the other person exactly what you think of them. At the time it feels as if it would be good to get everything you feel out in the open. The opposite is true. You will make the situation worse. You may feel better while you are saying how you feel but if it is in anger, it will not solve anything. Those who anger you, control you.

KNOW WHEN TO WALK AWAY

If you are feeling angry/upset and cannot handle the situation, try to walk away and take time out. There are many ways to do this:

- Physically remove yourself.
- Say that you prefer not to discuss the matter further at the moment.
- If on the phone, say you have to go but you will call back.

ACT ON FACTS NOT EMOTIONS

With family and other situations emotions can surface blurring the facts. You need to act on facts not emotions, however bad you may feel. See above (also see the exercise given in Post-Traumatic Stress Disorder).

PASSIVITY/TAKING IT ON THE CHIN

Know the difference.

Passivity means just letting things happen and not setting boundaries, so the other party thinks their behaviour is justified and acceptable.

Taking it on the chin means that you have made the decision not to take action. You know you could but you have decided on this occasion not to say or do anything. There are times when this behaviour is powerful.

RESPONSES

Family can feel they have the right to pass judgement. Learn non-aggressive responses.

Oh.

Oh, I'm sorry you don't approve.

I'm happy with ...

WORKPLACE BULLYING

- Common in every type of organisation.

- Keep a record of incidents. In a diary is a good idea so that you have dates and times. You could keep a separate diary at home specially to record incidents.

- Talk to someone you can trust. (Possibly outside of your organisation.)

- Recognise the first signs and *nip it in the bud.*

- Do not suffer in silence. There is help. It is not a sign of weakness to seek help.

- Bullying suffered in silence causes stress and ill health.

- Those being bullied at work are often good at their job and are being bullied for minor/petty mistakes which takes away their confidence and leads to further errors.

- You will cease to suffer from bullying once you recognise the first signs, set boundaries by standing up to the bully in an assertive and confident manner.

- Once it has taken a hold it is more difficult to deal with. Sometimes reporting it can be ineffective which has an even more negative effect on the victim; that is why it is important to seek professional help outside of the organisation.

- Don't expect the bully to be disciplined or dismissed. Unless the behaviour is physical or extreme, most get away with it and victims need to accept that fact and learn how to deal effectively with bullies.

- Some organisations run workshops on Dealing with Difficult Behaviour (bullying) because they know it is easier to teach employees how to deal with it than to deal with complaints, which in most cases fail:

  o Victims talk more about the emotions than the plain facts.

  o It is harder to respond to emotions than deal with facts.

  o What is bullying to one person is no more than irritating behaviour to another.

  o Unrealistic expectations on how the bully should be disciplined.

- If you report bullying do it in a non-emotional manner. People can find it difficult to respond to emotions. If you can report in a calm manner, you are more likely to be listened to.

- Identify the behaviour rather than use the word *bullying*. *Targeted* sounds powerful. *I have been targeted and here is the evidence.*

- Back up your complaint with evidence; incidents, dates and times. Copies of emails.

- Some make the choice to leave an organisation because life is too short to suffer under a bully. They seldom feel a failure for leaving. They know whether or not the system will back them and they would rather avoid the stress. It is a choice.

SCHOOL BULLYING

If you are being bullied at school:

o Tell your parents as soon as it happens, or someone whom you can trust. You do not have to go through this alone.

o Aim to be in the company of a friend whom you can trust, especially when leaving the school premises.

o You are not alone, it happens to thousands of school children.

o You can discuss the options with an adult. Once you have told someone you will feel better.

o You will recover as a stronger person.

o If you are being bullied online, (social media sites) through texts or emails, discuss with someone changing your email address or mobile number. Remove yourself from social media for a while. This is one place where you can be in control. If you choose not to read the rubbish, then you are in control. Those who bully through technology are cowards.

If your child is being bullied at school:

• Calmly listen to your child.

• Do not overreact; they need you to be strong.

• Give them reassurance that it will be dealt with and depending on the age of the child, you can discuss with them the options.

• If you report it to the school, make sure you list the behaviour and not just say that your child is being bullied.

• List dates, times and incidents.

• Calmly ask the school what they are going to do about it.

- Engage your child in activities outside of school which increases their self-confidence.

- Treat it as calmly as you can. Getting angry will only worsen the situation.

- Aim to work with the school in resolving the situation. Example: *How can we stop this, not only for my child but for others?*

- Do not automatically expect the school to deal with the situation. They, of course, should but many schools do not know how to deal with bullying and prefer to deny it is happening within their own establishment. Help them to help you, other children and parents.

- If you get no support from the school, seek outside advice.

- Keep a watchful eye on your child without being over-protective. Teenagers can feel embarrassed about being bullied and may not tell their parents.

- Love, support, distraction, fun activities will help everyone in the family cope with the unpleasant situation.

- Victims of bullying feel they have done something wrong or they are not liked. Reassure them that people bully, not because they *don't like you* but, because they don't like themselves.

- Reassure not to take it personally. Bullies need an easy target, that is why they choose kind, gentle people who will not fight back. Be careful how you phrase this. It depends on the age of the child. You don't want your child thinking it is their fault for being a nice person.

We will never eradicate bullying because it depends on how the victim views it and manages it. It comes in so many forms, some children cope better than others. What we can do is support and teach children how to manage it.

All teachers need to be aware and keep a careful watch on their students to see that they are free to learn in a safe environment whatever their age.

Many adults never forget the bullying they experienced as a child. If this is happening to you, seek help to let go of the past. Bullies usually don't remember their victims because it was not personal. They needed a victim and they needed someone who would not fight back, an easy target. If it was not you, it would have been someone else.

DIFFICULT FAMILY MEMBERS

In most families there is at least one who displays difficult behaviour. Learn to understand and manage the behaviour.

Family get-togethers can be especially difficult. Getting uptight and angry makes things worse. If you know you are going to meet with a member of the family who is difficult put a plan in place beforehand and you may find you will not need it. Family know how to get a reaction. No reaction is the best form of reaction because it stops the behaviour. If there is no reaction, then there is no point in being difficult.

A few tips:

- Don't take the behaviour personally, even if it does seem to be directed at you.
- Take a deep breath and pause before you respond.
- Keep calm and in control.
- Behave with dignity. You will feel better if you do.
- Read the section on PTSD.

COMMON REASONS FOR FAMILY DIFFICULTIES

- Jealousy
- The past
- Finance
- Sibling rivalry
- In laws/extended family
- Different expectations on disciplining of children
- Misunderstanding
- Lack of effective communication skills
- Age differences
- Lack of respect
- Lack of interpersonal skills
- Differing expectations
- Perceived lack of gratitude
- Non-forgiveness

Now we are in an age of texting and emails, it is easier for a misunderstanding to occur. Tone of voice alters the written word. It can depend on how you read a text or email or how you interpret it. When you are feeling upset by a text/email, leave it as long as possible before replying. Reply when you feel calmer. Write your reply and then read it at least twice to ensure you are comfortable with it. Read what you have written out loud and see how it sounds. Not just in families but in business too there are many regrets with texts and emails, you cannot retract the written word. In many cases it may be preferable to speak directly to the person. Body language and tone of voice play an important part in communication.

Just because you are family does not necessarily mean you have to get along. You can choose your friends but you cannot choose your family. Family is important and making life as nice as possible for everyone, whilst setting and respecting boundaries is a diplomacy which will pay worthwhile dividends.

FAMILY DISPUTES

Disputes within families run deep and cause major stresses and anxiety. People will often say things to family members they wouldn't dream of saying to friends and acquaintances. Grudges go way back. However, if resolution is sought, often stronger relationships are formed because of the family bond. A present day difference can trigger all the past problems, bringing back buried emotions and it is important to realise this is what happens with family problems.

- Treat your family with the respect you treat others in your life. Even if it is not returned.

- If problems are too monumental to solve then seek family mediation.

- Try not to take bad behaviour personally, it may be that family member is holding onto a grudge. You cannot change them but you can change your reaction to their behaviour.

- If you are able to talk problems through and move on, then everyone benefits.

- Use the non-personalising rule and try to see situations from the other person's perspective.

- Family events where several generations are thrown together can be stressful. Try to plan in advance so everyone is considered. Older people and the very young need regular meal times. A hungry person is not a happy person.

- Always criticise the behaviour not the person. Make sure your family always know they are loved even if you may not approve of their behaviour at times.

- Not all families get on; it is sad but sometimes it is easier just to accept the fact and manage family get-togethers as best you can.

- Respect, integrity, fairness, trust and kindness are all important ingredients for a happy family environment.

- Let go of the past and move on in a positive way. Be the one to steer the family on a more positive path.

TOXIC FRIENDSHIPS

It was interesting just how many of my students had friendships that were toxic but never thought to end them. However bad the friendship they felt they would be wrong to end it.

Friendships can turn toxic if boundaries are not set at the beginning.

Mostly friendships are based on similar values to your own. It is said you can tell what a person is like by the friends they keep.

Exercise

If you picture your friends together in a room, how would someone judge you just on your friends?

Good friends:

- Enjoy a friendship on an equal basis.
- Support one another in good times and bad.
- Have a friendship built on trust.
- Never betray confidences.
- Only offer advice if asked.
- Respect boundaries.
- Have similar values.
- Are stimulating company.

If you have friendships that are no longer nurturing and are causing anxiety, don't be afraid to end them. You can do this gradually; it doesn't have to be brutal. Fewer texts, phone calls, meetings. If you are asked why, be careful not to lie. You could arrange to meet for a coffee but time cap it. If they don't respect that then it is even more reason to let go of the friendship. Some friends who are needy may feel rejected and then pressurise you because they don't want to feel rejected. That is no basis for a friendship.

You could have a policy with new friendships of *three strikes and the friendship is over.* The first time you get a warning that their values are different, you can call it a first strike. Maybe they let you down on a meeting or didn't repay a small loan. The second time reinforces the first and the third time tells you it is time to move on.

Quote by Stephen King:

> *Fool me once, shame on you.*
> *Fool me twice, shame on me.*
> *Fool me three times, shame on you and me.*

Or my interpretation:

> The first time it happens:
>   shame on them.
> The second time:
>   shame on them and me.
> The third time:
>   shame on me for allowing it to happen.

You could decide on which rule/explanation you will adopt.

Remember to be kind when you let go of a toxic friendship.

Just because someone has different values from yours, does not necessarily make them a bad person, it means you may not be compatible in a friendship.

DIFFICULT CONVERSATIONS

RESPOND, DON'T REACT

There should be a space between stimulus and response Frankl.

- Listen 100% to what the other person says.
- Don't interrupt.
- Let them finish.
- Pause, take a deep breath. It will increase your confidence.
- Respond.
- Aim to achieve win/win.
- Get your message across in 30 seconds or less.
- Ensure the other person is listening.
- Use clear, honest dialogue.
- Check on understanding.
- Allow silences.
- If the other person interrupts, stop talking.
- Or, say, *please let me finish.*
- End on a positive note.

LISTENING SKILLS

- The most important part of conversing is listening.
- Most of us are too busy thinking about what we will say next instead of listening fully to what is being said.
- If face to face, observe body language: does the body language re-enforce what is being said?
- Is the body language open or closed?
- If on the phone or in a meeting, write down key words.
- Feed back key words, this shows you are listening.
- Listen more than you speak.
- Know when to speak and when to remain silent.
- People like to be listened to.
- Listening is different from hearing.
- Listening means focusing on what is being said.
- Listening requires concentration.
- Successful people have excellent listening skills because knowledge is power and you learn so much from listening to all that is said.
- Listen for what is not being said.
- Observe what is being left out.
- People will get to the point sooner if you listen without speaking or nodding.
- Do not *listen, waiting to speak.*
- Many people are so eager to speak themselves that they fail to listen fully to what the other person is saying.
- Encourage the speaker to continue so that you obtain all the information you need.

ASSERTIVE BODY LANGUAGE

Your thoughts create your body language. If your thoughts are positive, it will reflect in your body language. If your thoughts are negative/angry/passive, others will be reading those thoughts through your body language.

Assertive body language is non-threatening and conducive to positive communication.

Open body language invites positive communication and the people with whom you are communicating will feel comfortable.

Body language backs up and gives credence to the words you are speaking.

WE GET TREATED THE WAY WE ALLOW OURSELVES TO BE TREATED

Be clear on how you want to be treated, especially in relationships.

At the start of a relationship it is important to employ excellent listening skills, not only will it make you appear more attractive, it will give you valuable information about the other person.

You need to make it clear that if you are treated less than you deserve then the relationship ends. By setting clear boundaries the other person knows exactly what would happen if they are unfaithful, untruthful, abusive or display any form of unacceptable behaviour.

At work, you need to be sure of your boundaries and not allow people to cross them.

Do not allow anyone to treat you with less respect than you deserve. It shows that you value who you are.

RESPONDING TO INTRUSIVE/PERSONAL QUESTIONS

These questions mostly start with *why?*

Experiment with these phrases and choose those that work for you:

I would prefer not to discuss that.
I am interested why you ask that?
I'm not prepared to discuss this.
I am uncomfortable discussing this.
Forgive me, but I would rather not discuss this.
This is something I am not happy talking about.

Then move on with a different conversation in order that all parties do not feel uncomfortable.

DEALING WITH PEOPLE YOU CAN'T STAND

- It is going to happen. We cannot like everyone we come into contact with but we can behave in a respectful and assertive manner.

- See the situation from their side. It does help in how you behave towards them.

- Use all the assertiveness skills you have learnt.

- Be polite, but not over-friendly.

- Ensure your boundaries are in place.

- If you are in a position of authority, make sure you are fair and this person is treated the same as others.

NEIGHBOUR DISPUTES

The emotions with neighbour disputes run high. Neighbour disputes cause a great deal of serious stress. This is an area where literally and figuratively you need to get boundaries in place.

You don't have to like your neighbours but you do have to co-exist in harmony if you want stress-free living. Holding grudges will do more harm than good.

By being a good, kind, considerate neighbour you should find it easier to attract like for like, but not always.

Golden Rules

- Nip in the bud any potential disputes. Avoid avoidance, deal with matters as soon as they arise.

- By nipping things in the bud it saves disputes showing up on your property records.

- Get to know your neighbours; you don't have to be in and out of each other's houses, just polite conversation.

- Communicate politely.

- Start conversations with *How can we resolve this?*

- Complaining and whingeing will set up barriers.

- Be friendly towards your neighbours, it makes life easier if there is a problem.

- Be thoughtful, let them know in advance if you are having building works carried out or late parties.

- Always think win/win.

- However angry you feel, still look for a way of resolving potential problems.

- Neighbours get uptight about boundaries, even if an inch of their land is taken by a badly positioned fence or wall. It is worth noting so that you instruct workmen accordingly. By a different tac, if they take an inch of your land ask yourself if it is worth the hassle and stress of creating a dispute.

- Don't be too accommodating. Be professional and act in an assertive manner otherwise you could be giving them permission to take advantage.

- Always remain calm and polite, however badly the other party acts. Good manners, being calm and polite, acting with integrity are powerful tools when dealing with difficult neighbours.

- Before confronting a neighbour about a problem, write down the facts and the outcome you would like. Only approach them when you are calm.

  Example: *When you have a moment could we discuss the parking problem and find a resolution?*

- Welcoming new neighbours when they move into your area with an offer of tea (or wine) sets the scene for harmony. People will tolerate much more if neighbours are pleasant. They may overlook a noisy dog or boisterous noisy children if there is mutual like and respect.

- End on a positive note. *Thank you for your consideration on this.*

- Move on from a disagreement as quickly as possible, however angry you feel.

One of the main reasons relations with neighbours break down, is that people don't know how to deal with matters assertively. They are either aggressive which closes down communication or passive and withdraw so nothing gets resolved.

A large van was regularly parking perfectly legally near my own property but I couldn't see to get out of my drive so I put the following notice on the windscreen.

Please could I ask you nicely not to park here as I cannot see to drive in or out of my property and I am concerned in the case of safety of a child, an elderly person or a cyclist. Thank you.

The van never parked there again. (When relating this story, I am criticised for being over polite, but I got a result so it is worth every bit of politeness.)

You can choose your friends but you cannot choose your neighbours. Lawyers get rich on neighbour disputes.

There is a lot of sense in the phrase *love thy neighbour.*

AVOID DUPLICITY

Duplicity – in this case – talking about people behind their back.

It happens everywhere. Be the person *who stands outside the pack.* Don't join in, however much you may want to. If a group is discussing someone behind their back, you know what will happen when you are not present.

This is especially important if you want to be successful in the workplace. Be known as someone who does not talk about people when they are not there or indulges in gossip.

If a colleague or manager has annoyed you, it is natural to want to discuss it. Try to tell someone outside of work.

In or out of work, avoid talking about people in an unkind way in their absence. People will soon realise when you don't join in and will respect you because they know you will not be doing it about them.

You could say *I can't comment because this person is not here to defend themselves.*

TEMPORARY LOSS OF COMPETENCY

The most competent of people can experience an attack whereby they lose their confidence and even the simplest of tasks produces errors. Some causes:

- Constant criticism
- Major stressful life events
- Overwork
- Lack of sleep
- Ill health

When this happens the person will believe they are no good. It can cause panic attacks.

An example could be a teacher having been criticised for making a spelling mistake on the board. They would feel so embarrassed and humiliated and then try hard not to make further mistakes but in fact go on to make several more.

This can happen to anyone under pressure.

Confident people have confidence in their abilities and will just brush it off. The less confident, who may have a tendency towards perfectionism, will find it hard to cope with their mistakes.

If this happens to you, take a break. A few minutes or a few days depending on how acute the stress is:

- Practise meditation
- Exercise
- Do some relaxing activities
- Have some fun
- Get everything into perspective
- Take a lighter approach, be easier on yourself

You will find your confidence returns and you are able to function at your normal level.

USEFUL ASSERTIVE PHRASES

Practise these in a clear calm voice:

- *I can see you are angry/upset, shall we discuss this another time?*
- *I need ...*
- *Are you saying ...?*
- *Forgive me if I have got this wrong ...?*
- *The situation looks like this to me, is this right?*
- *Shall we explore what went wrong and find a solution?*
- *I am pleased we have discussed this.*
- *Am I right in thinking?*
- *Have I understood this correctly?*
- *Can we negotiate a solution?*
- *What would you do in my position?*
- *What is the outcome you are looking for?*
- *How can we achieve win/win?*

A MISCELLANY OF FREQUENTLY REQUESTED TOPICS

LOVE

Knowing we are loved is a very basic human need. What does love mean to you?

Many students attend courses following the break up of a relationship and are not sure what they are looking for regards love.

Before answering the above question. Make a list of what love is not.

By looking at your list you can see what you may need to learn about love. A student told the class that she frequently teased her new partner and couldn't understand why he felt hurt. As a child she was constantly teased by her father and her mother told her it was a sign of love. She was teased all her life by men and she thought it was funny and a sign of love until that teasing one day turned into something much nastier (psychopathic bullying). She had missed the early signs. Teasing is not love. Sharing a sense of humour and laughing together is part of a healthy relationship.

How we are loved as children has an impact on our adult relationships.

LOVE IS NOT:

- Controlling.
- Angry.
- Manipulative.
- Jealous.
- Cold.
- Expecting the other person to love you in the way you want without telling them.
- Unkind/hurtful.
- Aggressive.

- Being needy.
- Relying on the other person for your happiness.
- Playing mind games.

LOVE IS:

- Unconditional.
- Supportive.
- Gentle, kind and caring.
- Fun.
- Passionate and intense.
- Trusting.
- Forgiving and forgetting.
- Not bearing a grudge.
- Respectful.
- Truthful.
- Dignified.
- Faithful.
- Being able to tell your partner if you feel hurt by their behaviour.
- Supporting each other's growth.
- Being soul-mates.

Can you add to the list?

You may need to communicate your needs to your partner; let them know what is important to you.

Hold on too tightly to love and it is like grasping water, it slips away. Being needy and possessive is not love. It is said the only love you keep is the love you give away.

COPING WITH THE END OF A RELATIONSHIP

Relationships end for many reasons and in different ways. The one I am most asked to help with is when students have a prior feeling the other party is going to end the relationship.

It rarely comes as a complete surprise when someone ends a relationship. There are clues which you hope you are misreading.

A relationship is over when one person says it is. If the other party is not communicating clearly, take control and ask them if it is over.

If your partner is asking for space. Let them have it. (There is often someone else in that space, but not always.) It gives the other party time to think and reflect on the relationship they had with you, whether or not there is somebody else.

Once you know it is over handle it with dignity. Wish them every happiness, despite how awful you feel. If you truly love someone their happiness should be important to you even if it means that happiness is without you. Be proud that you acted with dignity.

Wish them well and *go*. Do not hang around for difficult conversations. Take time and space before discussing the practical side of the break-up. However, hurt you feel, the more dignity you can display at the time of the break-up the easier it will be for you to move on and discuss the practical side, especially if children are involved. They need to see their parents coping in a dignified manner.

The end of a relationship is like a bereavement, here are some tips:

- Do not grieve for too long, you need to get on with your life.
- Accept, let go, move on.
- Be careful of starting a new relationship until you are ready and have let go of the old one.
- See it as an opportunity to start a new life.
- Learning to cope on your own will make you stronger for the

next relationship.
- Look for the lessons you learnt during the relationship and the break-up.
- If your partner has moved on with someone new, you need to let go and move on yourself. There is no benefit in bearing or holding onto grudges. It will only harm you, not them.
- The stages you may have to go through are: anger, grief, acceptance, letting go.
- Do not blame yourself.
- You can get over it, millions of people do, so don't view it as rejection.
- If the pain feels too much to bear then seek professional help. You may benefit from some counselling.
- Do not expect immediately to get over the break-up of a relationship, it needs the appropriate amount of time.
- Look at it as an opportunity to grow, learn and enjoy new things.
- Resist contacting your ex unless it is extremely urgent or children are involved. Making contact puts the other person in control of how they act. Showing that you have taken it well and moved on is very attractive and you will feel dignified and confident.
- If you feel like taking revenge, then the best revenge you can take is to pick yourself up, accept, let go and move on with confidence.

Saying *No* To Being Asked for a Date

Because of your own fear of rejection you may find it difficult saying *no* to new relationships. It requires clear, honest, dialogue so the other person is not given the wrong message. If you are not interested, do not be afraid to say in a calm and kind way *No, thank you, I can't, but thank you for asking me.* That should be enough, however if they persist, just repeat what you said the first time.

It is kinder to deliver the message clearly and assertively. By being honest and direct you will minimise embarrassment. If you have been on a date(s) and you are asked for another, you could say *thank you, but this isn't working for me.*

WHY CONTACTING *HIM* ISN'T A GOOD IDEA

Sorry guys but this is one of the questions I get asked most often by women, especially when they start dating again after a relationship break-up.

He hasn't rung, is it all right for me to ring him?

I then ask what they think my answer will be. (They hate that response because they know what it will be.) An absolute *NO*.

If he hasn't rung it could be for a variety of reasons but mostly because he didn't want to.

Here are some facts:

- Men will often say after a first date, *I will ring you*. It is just a phrase, like *see you around*. They may not have the courage to say they don't want another date.

- By ringing it shows you are keen and most men like to do the chasing.

- Appearing too keen is not attractive.

- Why set yourself up for *rejection*.

- If a man is busy he usually doesn't want to be disturbed so if you ring at the wrong time it may sound like a brush off.

- However modern and liberated women have become, most men still like to do the chasing.

- Men are not that shy. They will ring if they want to.

- The reason women with a low self-esteem want to ring men after a date is to prevent the pain of feeling rejected and they want reassurance everything is *all right*. Work on coping with the fear of rejection. Distract yourself and be pleasantly surprised if he does ring.

- The women who have ignored my advice on this have regretted it.

Apologies to the men reading this book and to those in same sex relationships. (Please contact me with your views if you feel offended by what I have said.)

TRUST

How can I learn to trust again?

- Learn to trust yourself first.

- You cannot guarantee someone will be faithful but you can set boundaries on what you will and will not accept in a relationship. This needs to be done from the beginning.

- If you are clear in your own mind that if someone was unfaithful, or lied to you, that would be the end of the relationship, then you have boundaries in place.

- Confident people do not allow people in their lives whom they cannot trust because it is emotionally draining to be with someone you do not trust.

- Be confident in putting your own needs first. If you meet someone and feel you cannot trust them, then trust yourself to either discuss your fears in a non-accusative manner or end the relationship.

- Do not check up on the other person, by looking at their phone, Facebook, following them, etc. It is an invasion of their privacy. This is moving into stalking territory.

- Trust has to be earned, look at your list of values and make a list of values you expect (and would not compromise) in a partner. If they do not have those values, you may be better off out of the relationship.

- Be confident that you would be better off on your own than with a partner whom you cannot trust.

- Build trust in yourself and your own judgement.

BEAUTIFUL OUTSIDE/UGLY INSIDE

The best facelift is a smile.

A common statement by students, that they may look smart and attractive but inside they feel ugly. Feeling beautiful on the inside is more important than stunning good looks. People who are beautiful inside radiate on the outside.

Feeling ugly inside is normally due to childhood messages, which have formed the self-esteem. In class, no amount of times the other students tell them how attractive they are alters their belief. This has to be worked on (see self-esteem section).

Bullying causes people to feel ugly.

Apart from good general grooming, confident people are not obsessed by how they look. They are far more interested in other people and what is going on in the world. That is what makes them attractive.

Think before embarking on plastic surgery. It may fix a problem for a short while but the low self-esteem will return and then it is back for more surgery.

Before considering cosmetic surgery, work on your self-esteem and then decide whether you need the surgery.

- Walk with confidence (good posture).
- Walk tall, imagine you are a model.
- Reaching out to others and being kind will enhance your confidence.
- Happy people are those who give to/care for others. It is the route to happiness and happy people are attractive.
- Put the past behind you and enjoy the here and now.
- Affirm to yourself:
  - *I am good enough/happy with the way I look.*

HOW TO BE A BEAUTIFUL PERSON

Think of someone you know who is a beautiful person. List what it is about them that makes them beautiful.

Beautiful people are:

- Loving
- Kind
- Supportive
- Thoughtful
- Considerate
- Not self-obsessed
- Interested in others
- Compassionate
- Non-judgemental
- Non duplicitous
- Non-critical

The main quality about people with a beautiful personality is that they are not wrapped up in themselves; they reach out to, and are interested in, others.

LONELINESS

Feeling lonely and isolated is serious and needs to be addressed. If you are feeling lonely for whatever reason take steps to overcome it.

It may just be a feeling that is linked to depression. If so, you may need to seek professional help.

What is causing your loneliness?

If you mix with other people, there is little chance of being lonely. Think about what you can do to address your loneliness:

- Voluntary work.
- Invite friends for coffee/supper.
- Join clubs.
- Learn new skills.
- Join a place of worship.
- Be part of a sports/quiz team.
- Get involved in community work.
- Start a book club.
- Go to evening classes.
- Join a gym.

You need to make the first move in meeting people. You cannot rely on people coming forward to meet you. It takes confidence and you need to be sure of your safety.

Going on social media websites will not cure loneliness. You may have thousands of *friends* on social media sites but it is not the same as face to face contact. We all need human contact.

Exercise

- Make a list of all the people in your life who care about you.
- Contact one of those people by phone, text or email to enquire how they are.
- Plan ahead social activities where you can meet new people.
- Make a list of 40 ways to meet new people. You don't need to follow all of them but it will get you thinking laterally.
- Is there an elderly neighbour you could offer to help?
- Charity events can be a fun way to meet new people.

Stepping out of loneliness means reaching out to others.

TIPS FOR SUPPORTING SOMEONE WITH LOW MOOD/DEPRESSION OR PTSD

Students ask how they can help family members and friends when they are going through a difficult time and suffering from low mood or depression:

This is general, not specific, as every situation is different.

- Ask how you can best help them.
- Support. Don't judge or enquire why they feel the way they do.
- Listen. Only give advice if asked and preface advice with *if it was me I would …*
- Keep a watchful eye in case their situation goes on for too long or gets worse, then suggest professional medical help.
- Be prepared for negativity. Listen.
- Walking is great exercise for low mood. Suggest accompanying them on a walk.
- Suggest going out for coffee.
- Support their recovery.
- Look after yourself. Know when to stand back.
- Small acts of kindness.
- Depression isolates and causes loneliness so just being there may be enough.
- Validate feelings, don't minimise situations. People who are depressed may overreact to situations they would normally take in their stride. Avoid rationalising. Use phrases such as:
  - *I can see that has upset you.*
  - *That is hurtful/stressful.*
  - *Is there anything I can do to help?*

POST-TRAUMATIC STRESS DISORDER

This is a disorder where certain situations trigger past memories and feelings. A type of this disorder can occur with family get-togethers. Someone says or does something to offend and past history will come to the fore with accompanying feelings. If this happens to you, learn to recognise it. It may appear, to others, that you overreact to fairly innocuous situations. The explanation is that all the past memories have been triggered together with the feelings you had at the time.

Learn how to deal just with the facts and not mistake the feelings as facts. One way is to take a sheet of paper and divide it in two. On one half write all your feelings. On the other half write only the facts: not what you think is happening but the basic facts. This will help you deal with the present situation and not include the past hurts.

The more you do this, the more confident you will become.

MANAGING RELAPSES

It is hoped you will gain many new skills from experimenting with the exercises in this book. It takes 21 days to form a new habit so be patient with your progress.

Expect relapses; they are inevitable. Students get despondent when they suffer a loss of confidence or they fail to respond assertively in a situation.

You can never go back to how you were. You have learnt new skills; you may suffer a setback but it will be different and now you have the tools to re-build your confidence.

Much of this learning is based on experimenting with what works for you. There can be many reasons for a relapse:

- Stress.
- Illness.
- Change of job.
- Bereavement.
- Moving from school to university.
- Leaving university.
- Moving away from home.
- Moving home.
- Getting married/having a baby.
- Divorce.

When we are feeling confident and happy we tend not to want to revisit how we once felt and then it comes as a shock when a relapse occurs. It is useful while you are working through this book to make a personal plan for a relapse, keep it with the book.

Keep this book where you can easily find it, together with your notes and the plan to cope with your relapse.

When you experience success in your personal development ensure you write about it in your journal. You will want to do more of what works for you.

Do not feel a failure because you are having a relapse. It is all part of your continuing growth.

When you suffer a relapse the first areas to check are:

- Exercise.
- Diet.
- Sleep.

When stressed these are the first areas that suffer. By just putting these in place again, you may find that is all you need to do. But do have a plan in place.

Mindfulness and Cognitive Behavioural Therapy (MCBT) is now recommended by the NHS as opposed to anti-depressants. You would need to discuss with your GP if your setback continued for longer than a couple of weeks.

It is important that all new learning goes from the short term memory (STM) to the long term memory (LTM) and that is why you may just need more practice at some of the exercises.

You cannot expect to change overnight. You will see a change in your confidence when you first start the exercises and this is exciting so it can be disappointing to have a setback.

Welcome a setback because it gives you more chance to recover even stronger.

Teaching others some of the lessons you have learnt will help reinforce your own learning (however be careful only to offer advice, when asked).

By embracing a setback and not fearing it, you will recover quickly.

Especially with assertiveness, so many new situations will occur which you hadn't anticipated. Learn from them. You may not have handled the situation in the best way but look for the lesson you learnt and how you would do it differently next time.

FINDING HAPPINESS

Firstly you need to define what happiness means to you. The perfect life doesn't exist. Wealth doesn't bring happiness. Happiness comes from within. You cannot suddenly become happy because you have won the lottery, met a new partner, got a new car as examples. If you think you can, be assured that after six months your old thoughts and feelings will return.

If you want to be happy, start working on it today.

Discover what makes you happy and do more of what you enjoy.

Here are some suggestions:

- Look after your health: diet, exercise and sleep.
- Laughter is the best medicine.
- Live in the present moment whilst making some plans for the future.
- Work on peace of mind/serenity.
- Give out to others.
- Develop a healthy sense of humour.
- Never stop learning.
- Be well organised.
- Embrace and welcome change.
- Be self-sufficient.
- Enjoy art, music and literature.
- Be enthusiastic.
- Be grateful. Regularly list all that you are grateful for.
- Follow the exercises in this book.